Blue Dragon Press
Poetry Collection

SIGNS OF LIFE

by

BRENDA WHINCUP

©Brenda Whincup

First published in 1996 by
Blue Dragon Press Ltd.
2 Holly House, Rose Hill
Dorking, Surrey RH4 2EQ (UK)

All Rights Reserved

Bookbinding by Susan Kasper, Oxford
Printed by Hurtwood Litho
39a South Street, Dorking, Surrey RH4 2JX

Illustrated by ©Iris Coby

British Library Cataloguing-in-Publication Date
A Catalogue record for this book is available from
the British Library

ISBN 1 900365 09 X

FOR MY HUSBAND WITH LOVE

ACKNOWLEDGEMENTS
Some of these poems have appeared in Bucks and Berks, and the Herts Countryside magazines; Borderlines; Counterpoint; Master Craftsman; Possibility; Stratford Poets' III; Word Shop II and iii. The Aberdeen University Press, American Poetry Association., Forest Poets', Phoenix Poets', Poet's England and the SWWJ anthologies.

COMPETITIONS
'Requiem for the Mother's Child' was lst at Contra Costa, 1980
'Hallowe'en: 1980s'   gold medal at Cambridge, 1985
'Now Eighteen'   lst in Sutton Writers', 1992
'December Dusk'   "   "   Castle Poets', 1994

Signs of Life
by
Brenda Whincup

Illustrated
by
Iris Coby

Blue Dragon Press

SIGNS OF LIFE

Signs in Living

Signs in the Family

Signs from Sequences

Signs in Fun

Signs in Times and Places

SIGNS IN LIVING

SIGNS OF LIFE

Summer leaves behind a
rose to droop
its heavy head on slender
neck and drop
the last, precious petals
on the cooling earth

where the worm is coiled
around the root; both alive.

My hot-eyed days now slowly
turn their backs on
all the fragile dreams; but
even if this razor-edge
against my flesh draws
blood, and I
bleed as darkly as the rose

this too is a sign of life.

IDENTIFIED

(for Billy)

"Can't you see the
hand before your face?"

A question mark, lolling
against the edge
of the mirror, folded
its arms as
it demonstrated a smile.

A short-sighted glass
returned an empty
room—a closed door.

The knocking, when it
came, was gentle;
even so I
hardly dared to call
"Come in"
but still you entered

and at last I saw
my reflection
there, in your eyes ....

A LAMENT FOR BUTTERFLIES

I can't remember
hearing birds, that
summer. There were
flowers I know
they came, cut down
in full-bloom
to die, upon the new-
turned earth
of my mother's grave.

Her time had been
as brief
as shadows cast
by butterflies. Where

were the butterflies?

That summer ....

THE PASSION AND THE PAIN

The world grows tired, small
joys seem rare, and change
is changed too soon, too soon.
Our shadows pass upon the stair
and fill the empty room. But
it's lovely in the park
the painted horses fly around
the carousel as life and all
our dreams ride by. The passion
and the pain, my love, the scarlet
and the gold; life is warm
upon our skin, while time itself
grows cold. The passion and
the pain, my love, the fire and
the flame; the music plays forever
but, too soon, it fades away ....

LAST NIGHT I WAS TWENTY

veiled in a tissue of dreams
rosy, nubile, unashamed
I was twenty and my hair
was bound by ropes
of honeysuckle. The golden

chain around my neck hung
long, and cool, against
the naked heat of my breasts
flame-rouged by carnation.

Eve lit her lantern in my
eyes. My tongue tasted
nectar, was clumsy
in its searching—still

I was the moon incarnate.
Wild music. Rapture
with a pearl in her navel

and I remembered
the penetrating night when
the white rose opened
to the pain of total joy.

This morning, I brush the
cobwebs, in my hair; regret
the disguise of change—but
last night, I was twenty ....

JOSEPH: A CARPENTER

Should some cataclysmic
force, resurrect a man
whose very blood and bone
—quick, thrusting joy—
long ago became dust
in the weeping eye of time

what TERRORS would he
find illuminated by
our harsh, electric sun?

Unless it was the Nazarene
tooled, by his craft, to
a patience beyond belief,
willing, to accept the Lamb
of God, and nurture
a plant not of his seed.

He might be comforted that
the tools of his trade
are recognisable, yet,
across the lost centuries.

For what has there ever
been to time
when hand, and mind, are
concentrated on shaping
the forgiving wood in to
symbols of our philosophy?

FINAL CHAPTER FOR A BOOKWORM

I have always wanted
more than less. Unable
to rest when appetite
and dreams lead directly
to the stars. But
time moves, needs change;
today gold, tomorrow
grain, depending on who
and what we are. Still
it must come down to this:
just the basic gift of
being part of time and all
its hurry. Until the final
place, where my bookmark
has to rest, and I hope
it's at the end of a story.

SIGNS IN THE FAMILY

A TOUCH OF GRACE
(for my mother-in-law)

I know you. You are
one of the four
images of excellence.

Last of
the shadows cast, by

the child; young love;
everywoman as Madonna
and Joan, together
Still, with Darby
in their quiet harbour.

I see you lingering
in the park
with birds, like
memories
of children,
around your feet

and, if the shallow
winter sun is
brief, it brings a
faded rose to your
parchment, gilding
a diagram that
delineates
all paths to peace.

The years, windfalls
in your lap.
I call you Mystery.

AFRICAN VIOLETS

She loved their candid faces—
open, simple
shapes, well within the compass
of a child's crayon—their
colour, holding all that's blue
of blue until it spills in glory.

The shade became her well, she

wore it for my wedding; mother
of the bride, shy and glowing
like her favourite flowers ....

I loved her candid
face—her blue, blue eyes.

CHRISTMAS PRESENCE
(Christmas Morning, 1961)

She came
just before the star-frosted shadows
fled from the sun and I,
in the awe that the living
have for the dead, was confused
as my grandmother's spirit asked me:
"Do you **know** how late it is?"

The thaw of the season brought a new
year in that saw
the death of my mother, and
remembering the Time of the Child
I came to understand
just how late it had been, then ....

TWO'S COMPANY
(for June)

I can see them now
those girls—
their bouffant skirts
and hair,
their moisturized, pearly
flesh; and never was
rose more red than their
colour-coded lips.

I can hear them now
those girls—
questioning the years:
"Will there be rainbows
and butterfly-dreams;
mystery, moonlight,
golden rings?" One
considered fame—the other
just yearned to be thin.

So, who are they now
those 'girls'?
Women more grey than pearl.
Each one wears contentment
they've shaped the game;
while, in the truth
of time, they remain
the very best of friends.

I will always remember
those girls ....

BLOGGS

It seems, to me, he prays.
Paws stretched out towards
the fire—pads, pink
as an infant rose;
scimitar claws silk-sheathed.

It is winter

and, perhaps, he dreams of
spring and a cat's cradle in
the fragrant arms
of apple trees—blossom
white as the patches patched
in to his witch-black fur.

He stirs and, perhaps, he
sees—one-eyed only, when
awake—the deep
adventuring summer green;
the autumn leaves
he plays with still, as
though he were a kitten-cat.

But it's winter

and safe before the fire
he dreams; or
as it often seems
to me, he says his prayers.

MY ROSE

(for Joan)

I would have named her Rose.
A perennial, she is
for me, without thorn or
blemish. A golden
long-stemmed beauty, her
flori-bundant giving
fills my room with perfume.
I would have named her Rose.

NOW EIGHTEEN
(for Tracey)

Girl, you are music.
The morning and the evening
star. You are the rosy
flowering heart of spring;
the emerald fire of summer.
You are the tremulous hush
just before a young bird
finds his song; a long, cool
drink of clear, fresh water.

You are our hearts' blood
Girl, we love you.

WINTER-SET
(for Billy)

My reflection, inside out
watches as I close
the curtains on an early dusk

leaving a black-winged night
to roost, in the thin
cold arms of a sycamore.

My shadow narrows back
into the room, as
a lonely wind insinuates
itself around the door
to haunt the house—across
each creaking board. But
lamp and flame are blended
in a Midas touch, and

with your footsteps echoing
home, the kettle sings.

SIGNS FROM SEQUENCES

LITTLE WOMEN
Julie
Tracey

HOSPITAL RECORDS
Transparency
Insomnia

DIAGRAMS OF PAIN AND FEAR
Apprehension
Trepidation

LITTLE WOMEN
-Julie-

Trembling on the tiptoed edge
of the child's wild
wondrous wood, you now
look upon
spring's flori-bundant meadow

your eyes soft with the dreams
I can no longer remember.

Lovely girl
as slender as the lily; your
pale hands could hold
butterflies, small birds,
leaving no bruise
to mark these timid things.

Linger among the primroses
opening their creamy
faces, in trust, towards you.
Always shine your
own clear face upon my world.

LITTLE WOMEN
-Tracey-

I rejoice to see your bright
marigolden head
turned towards the morning.

I feel the pull of the shadows
lying under the tree
but still your flame
warms the coldest, shrivelling
corners of my fear. I always
know where you've been,
for the earth opens its heart
to blossom all about you.

The peach is delicious
because it ripens under your
sun; the lark sings
because he knows your name;
and no briar, heavy
with bud to bursting, dares
to dream of possessing
such precious scent as yours.

You are beautiful.

HOSPITAL RECORDS

III: TRANSPARENCY

The plate glass view from this
bed, reflects such plenitude.
Brown bird—tumbling in self-
engrossed ecstasy—reveals
himself in all his shades,
from a neutrality barely warmed
to beige, deepening to brusk;
trees, submissive to an average
green, cool the dried-blood
burn of a copper beech; lilacs
grape and foam, scenting
a spring just out of reach.

Heavier, the breath of blossom
culled, as tribute
and comfort to the sick;
a tangle of colour, nullified
by a white-linen conformity.

HOSPITAL RECORDS

IV: INSOMNIA

Out there
a sense of foxes .... My window
receptive, wide, admits no
confirmation but every skulking
shadow, of this deep June night,
agrees there is a sense of foxes.

               In here
a private patch of light holds
the semblance of a tree,
twitching to its dreams; and
sleep, squatting in the corner,
disapproves
my quiet rebellion. But when

out there
there is a sense of foxes, red-
staining inocybe mushrooms
in the dark; witches conjure a
chaos of stairs; the elemental
heart beats
faster—with a sense of foxes.

DIAGRAMS OF PAIN AND FEAR

I: APPREHENSION

It is wisdom to hesitate, with
the key in the lock of the cage
that guards our needs 'I
wish ....' How easily this
dangerous phrase slips on the
tongue and turns us from reality.

Tarnished bars—once silver—
hold hope tame, and pleading
for release, again; while hiding
behind the vanquished years
a face, scarred by
humanity's proven fears and pain.

It is safer to hesitate, and
remove the key from the lock of
the cage. For hope, rampant
can undulate, shift, change shape
into a very different beast

spawned from a burnt-out star
a hydra, with a monkey's paw ....

DIAGRAMS OF PAIN AND FEAR

III: TREPIDATION

It doesn't change, the Waiting Room.
It is still a place where
the door's shut tight, and no
escape's allowed. Non-associating
time stops the clock, and dust
is thick upon the furnishings of our
normality. Instinct warns: 'Be still!'
Even though it seems the walls
move slowly inwards, forcing empty
hands to weave the stagnant
air into patterns of distress.

Somewhere an animal cry, articulate
of pain, is finally located as emanating
from my mind; and the Paternoster
fractures on my tongue, for Thy will
is not just good enough
when it's set against those we love.

Isolated is the only prayer:
strike blind the light, before I see
realization of my fears ....

SIGNS IN FUN

NEW TO ALL OF THIS

We eyed each other silently, over
six long years—a gift of
love that filled me with terror.
For, with a tendency towards
quill and vellum, new
technology—I feel—is a lemon.

So, better late—when I was sure
it would be never—I come
to know this Amstrad after all;
and find it, almost, to be human
sometimes with a mind of its own.

It's with the use of key f7—as
it checks my spelling out—when it
often puts me right and, with
Malapropian wisdom, gives
my thinking a wonderful new slant.

It has orgasms—I mean marked down
as proper spelling—although
with chastity, there is some doubt;
but enchantment, for me, is when
it makes suggestions
such as in the **freelance** of a rose.

In summer, the garden is 'fragment';
when cleaning, I might have
'recharged' the furniture around.
Life, can be amazing
described by an Amstrad, or a child.

THE PALE CAST OF THOUGHT
(Hamlet—Act 3: Scene 1)

My muse approaches slowly on
varicosed legs. Even the
ethereal must, it seems,
wither into age when
time stands on its dignity.

But—by Zeus—it is a
poor emolument when, finally
she staggers in,
bearing only paraphrase.

Granted she's been called
upon again, and again,
by those with a greater
authority than mine; but
even if she has me
labelled as second-rate
—or second-hand—
hardly is it fit, or kind

when, without asking if it
is, or not to be, she
tricks out the old with the
lewd; and, with a toothless
grin, she dribbles that:
"Coitus should be
made with a bare bodkin!"

The rest IS silence ....

SOMETHING IN THE ATTIC

Mr. Rochester kept a wife in his;
she was mad, and who can blame
her? Most people keep boxes
of letters in theirs, with bills
receipted as 'paid'. Dressing-up
clobber, swaddling baby's first
gear; a picture or two of Aunt Ada.

There has been the occasional Old
Master; vases, attributed to
Ming. By and large though, it's
lumber, of the most innocent kind.

We have an attic—with some boxes
of books in ours; cartons
of mementos; a rickety-rocky chair—
but we rarely feel the need to go
there except that, now, we are trying
to trace the source of noises
echoing through our cavity walls and

having found in the attic, signs of
something
that's coming and going, up there ....

WANTED: SPECIAL AGENT'

Rozinante is stabled
content, to wait;
after all hay is
more to his
taste, than windmills.

Don Quixote rests—where?

Is it right to even ask
when there have been
sturdier knights,
to resurrect.
Not that they
attached importance
to windmills. No wonder

the trade is obsolete!

And the increase
in windmills alarming.

PARKERING A COLLAGE
(with a nod towards Dorothy Parker)

There is always **e**nough **r**ope.

Sophistry urges us to breathe
a breath for hope. **N**ascent zeal
plants its **t**urnips while it may,
producing a fine winter crop
for sheep. Still, **t**hrenody is
but a thin **t**hread of **s**ong;
and my **c**lack does not distract
the **f**anfaronade of any colossus
who, in full **s**traddle,
manages to blow his own strumpet.

And many a persistent case of
cramp has been **s**hriven
in **s**able; under this
sky **of a**shes, that is
the way the cookie crumbles.

Truth deals in cold facts.
Bedight the waxen breast, with
the waxen flower, and finally
they share the same savour. Any
one who **l**imps this florid track
looking for by-**p**asses is
desperately in need, of **g**lasses.

SIGNS IN TIMES AND PLACES

HALLOWE'EN: 1980s

Wearing a clean, white apron

I will slit the bowel
of night, to dip my pointed
fingers in the bloated
black, extracting
all the ingredients I need.

The tongue of a woman, who
screamed 'Desolation'
as she jumped from a tower
block; the foreskin
from a man who hung himself
while searching for work;
entrails from a vivisected
dog the heart of
a baby battered to its death.

One by one, I will add these
morsels to a stock infused
from bones of those surplus
to any of a dozen different
wars. Softly, I will sing
as I stir my broth;
seasoning, with bitter
grasses, from earth scorched
beneath the invader's boot.

In my clean, bright kitchen

I will leave my familiar, who
answers to the name
of Progress, asleep before
the fire; and carefully
fold my apron, to leave it
neatly on a chair. Then, I
will skim the clotted curds—
from my shining, aluminium
vat—to anoint my secret
body; and it is then I will

unbraid
the whirlwind of my hair ....

REQUIEM FOR THE MOTHER'S CHILD
(after Dalton Trumbo's 'Johnny Got His Gun')

Your truth is pain, greater
than death, Johnny. The narrow
cot does promise oblivion, and you
featured in all the tortured
faces, know the comfort of that.

But, Johnny, the waste ....

They planted poppies in your eyes.
The bright, bitter petals spilt
and pooled, dousing your light—
we see the splintered space
of trees recycled into cruciform;
now that science is prepared
for its own begotten son to
reap all the flowers of the field.

You lost your chance of music.
We hear the clamouring of usury;
the discordancy
of madness giggling at its own joke.

Then what of hope—must it
be left to the knife, as the last
fit tool to scratch
the persistently itching crotch?

Ah, Johnny, to think

that in a world such as this
should be, there could
be, anything worse than death ....

DECEMBER DUSK
(Christmas Eve)

A troubled sky shifts
uneasily, gathering grey;
hoarding the bleak
imprint of a sycamore
 stripped to the bone
shivering
reaching to catch streamers
of cloud, opalescent
in a final dazzle of flame.

A bird, stunned
by a confusion of air,
supports its hesitation
with wings strained
in a ragged purchase
on space to spiral, within
the scope of elemental
grace, navigating
a true tack for home.

Rooks shout, a rough
goodnight. Wind
fidgets a whisper
through the dead, dried
rustle of shrub
and bush: "No moon,
no moon." Shadows, bleed
black, bandaging all
sense of time and place

as this primordial night
holds its breath, concealing
deep in its heart long
remembrance of light from
that one, enduring star ....

NOT ONE SHALL FALL
(Matthew: 10: 29)

*News item, August 1979: A sparrow
was destroyed when it disrupted
a music recital given in church.*

A child considers the cat
must taste of cream
and that is why
it licks itself, continually.

A sparrow considers music
is accessible as church
and so he
sings there, unrestrainedly.

A cat has only a sense of self
and the sport of birds;
a cleric with only a sense
of occasion and the intrusion
of birds, acts accordingly.

Men in all sorts of collars
bell the cat. Children, grow
up to sorrows, and to
disillusionment. Eventually.

JENNY SINGS
(For June and Bill, with me at Pimhill)

She has seen us first

her call, its note breaking to catch
like a sob in her throat, demands
our attention ...... "Hee-haw
Hee-haw"—do come quickly, look
I'm here—urges us to hurry
fast across the daisy-tangled grass.

My chair, wheels turned and locking,
stalls—as I wish, with all
my heart, these useless knees of mine
would, just once, let me run
to throw my arms around her neck—

and still Jenny sings
her wheezing, fractured greeting.

To this place we come
for organic-grown potatoes; new-baked
bread; lemon curd preserved
in sun-filled jars; picture postcards

and the chance of seeing Jenny.

OCTOBER IN EDEN
(Vale of Eden, Northumberland)

Above Eden I stood, transfixed
as summer nudged from sleep
encroaching autumn's lease
with one, brief, laughing day

that ran, careless
of the winter-waiting hills.

The constricted trace of human
racing stilled, cushioned
soft, on bracken; and my heart
was a small bird singing
high, in the bordering blue

unafraid, a single feather's
tip could touch eternity.

Free, fast-falling space
tumbled through light and air,
past crag and heath
to spread in a gesture of green
across the valley; but a sense
of ghosts trouble the earth
and there were tears
tasting of apples on my tongue.

Innocent was the flower crushed
underfoot as, at last, the day
turned to look at the hills
waiting—a grim night
and a burning moon—beyond Eden.

DAME-SCHOOL
(London, 1980)

I touch echoes in this house; beyond
the secret side of whisper
their frisson rubs gentle fingers
along the nerve. Coming here, our
choice was opted on an adventurous line
in arch and angle, the rounding of a
curve away from the blank-eyed
look of a four-squared preconception;
a persistence in time ....

Tonight we are alone, the house and I.

Sitting at the top of the stairs
looking down to the hall, its darkness
glow-wormed by a fanlighted door, I
watch a sullen space; listen, as
old boards stretch, crack, chain-react
in a furtive pit-a-patter: a scamper
of sound to remind me
that this house was, once, a school.

The shadows, now, watch me

and I wonder if one will dare describe
its own identity? The shape
is almost there: hair scrimped
its drab clay worn with a chatelaine
about the waist. But what if this
shadow, faking breath, should prove to
be just a little thing, itself afraid?

What would I do, if it came before me
in dimity, mob-cap and pinafore?
And, remembering I first came to this
house with a sense of returning
home, if it should also wear my face ... ?

INCOMERS
(to Shropshire in 1988)

We arrived with bags, baggage
and dreams, on a February
day when winter's
grip was gloved in iron;
yet there were lambs
in the fields, at our gate.

Three hard years have shambled
through the seasons as we
struggle, still, to restore
a much neglected house to fit
the scheme of things
that brought us to this shire.

Disappointment has been the salt
in our daily bread, then
comes a bee-stung summer's
morning
with honey on its breath;
the foxy autumn nights
beneath a razzle-dazzle moon

and, always on the very edge
of winter's grim estate lambs
promising spring
in the fields, at our gate.

Growing, Changing......................Signs of Life

BRENDA WHINCUP is a Londoner who now lives in rural Shropshire with her husband, their cats, geese and peafowl. She has been a freelance writer, mainly poetry, for twenty-something years and was resident poet with the old Master Craftsman journal. Her work has been in a variety of magazines and anthologies both in the UK and USA, including Waltham Forest Arts Council publications and Viking/Penguin collections of humour. She has read her work on radio and takes part in public readings.

Awards include first place prizes at the Contra Costa County Fair (USA) 1977 and 1980; the Brentwood Writers' Ronald Blythe competition, 1980; gold medal in the Cambridge Festival's Write and Speak section, 1985; the SWWJ Theodora Roscoe/Vera Brittain cup for prose, 1990; the Wrekin Writers' competition, 1991; the Sutton writers' competition, 1992; the Beryl Lewin-mini-saga section-Memorial competition, 1993; the Castle Trust Poets' competition, 1994. She belongs to the London Writer group, the Society of Women Writers and Journalists, and the Anglo-Welsh Poetry Society.